YOU MUST REMEMBER THIS
1974

MILESTONES, MEMORIES,
TRIVIA AND FACTS, NEWS EVENTS,
PROMINENT PERSONALITIES &
SPORTS HIGHLIGHTS OF THE YEAR

TO :

FROM :

MESSAGE :

D1367590

™

PUBLISHED BY WARNER BOOKS

A TIME WARNER COMPANY

Warner Books, Inc.
1271 Avenue of the Americas
New York, New York 10020

Warner Treasures is a
trademark of Warner Books, Inc.

A Time Warner Company

DESIGN:
CAROL BOKUNIEWICZ DESIGN
PRINTED IN SINGAPORE
FIRST PRINTING : MAY 1995
10 9 8 7 6 5 4 3 2 1
ISBN: 0-446-91051-1

It was the year Richard Nixon and Watergate continued to dominate the American psyche. Beginning May 9, the House Judiciary committee held televised impeachment hearings against the president. He was charged with taking part in a conspiracy to obstruct justice, failure to fulfill his constitutional oath, and unconstitutional defiance of committee subpoenas. On August 5, Nixon admitted that he originated plans to have the FBI stop its investigation of the break-in for political reasons.

PRESIDENT NIXON RESIGNED ON AUGUST 9.

Newspaper heiress **PATTY HEARST** was kidnaped from her Berkeley, CA, home by a group calling itself the Symbionese Liberation Army. Two months later, in a taped message, she announced that she was joining the SLA of her own free will and changing her name to Tania. On April l5, Tania/Patty was photographed robbing a bank in San Francisco.

newsreel

IN BOSTON, FEDERAL TROOPS WERE CALLED IN TO QUELL VIOLENCE AFTER THE LOCAL SCHOOL COMMITTEE REJECTED A COURT-ORDERED BUSING PLAN FOR DESEGREGATION.

After cancer-causing chemicals were found in drinking water throughout the United States, the Safe Drinking Water Act set water pollution standards.

IN NORTHERN IRELAND, A GENERAL STRIKE
SPONSORED BY MILITANT PROTESTANTS
FORCED THE COLLAPSE OF THE CATHOLIC-
PROTESTANT COALITION GOVERNMENT.
ONCE AGAIN, THE BRITISH
TOOK OVER RULE.

international

headlines

**yitzhak rabin
succeeded
golda meir as
prime minister
of israel.**

In Portugal, the
army overthrew
the president
and ended the
dictatorial rule
that had marked
the government
for 25 years.

4

IN WEST GERMANY, HELMUT SCHMIDT BECAME CHANCELLOR AFTER WILLIE BRANDT RESIGNED AS THE RESULT OF A SPY SCANDAL.

YASIR ARAFAT

OF THE PALESTINE LIBERATION ORGANIZATION MADE INTERNATIONAL HEADLINES WHEN HE ADDRESSED THE UNITED NATIONS WITH A GUN STRAPPED TO HIS SIDE.

"Condo Fever"

SWEPT THE NATION. 40.3% OF ALL NEW HOUSING UNITS

FOR SALE IN METROPOLITAN AREAS WERE CONDOMINIUMS.

gadgets

Kitchen convenience took great leaps this year: **Toaster ovens** sold for $45. A payment of $36.95 got you a **self-stirring cordless electric saucepan.** A **Mister Coffee** coffeemaker went for $40.

IN DRUG RESEARCH, THE NEW ENGLAND JOURNAL OF MEDICINE ANNOUNCED THAT MEN WHO SMOKED LARGE QUANTITIES OF "POT" HAD LOWER LEVELS OF TESTOSTERONE. FEARING THEY'D END UP IN D CUPS, HORDES OF MALE POTHEADS KICKED THE HABIT.

cultural
milestones

A study released in March showed that more Americans than ever were trying bisexuality. The poll revealed that 12 percent of women and nearly 24 percent of men had bisexual encounters.

7

television

Early in the year, the Big Three networks promised to reduce the amount of violence in shows presented to the American public.

THE WALTONS premiered in second place on **CBS**, forever guaranteeing that smart alecks the world over would say **"GOOD NIGHT, JOHN BOY"** every time they said good-bye.

TOP TV SHOWS

1. "All in the Family" (CBS)

2. "The Waltons" (CBS)

3. "Sanford and Son" (NBC)

4. "M*A*S*H" (CBS)

5. "Hawaii Five-O" (CBS)

6. "Maude" (CBS)

7. "Kojak" and

   "The Sonny and Cher Show," tie (CBS)

8. "The Mary Tyler Moore Show" and

   "Cannon," tie (CBS)

ACTION-BASED HOUR-LONG DRAMAS, WHICH HAD DOMINATED MOST OF THE NIELSENS FOR THE EARLY SEVENTIES, BEGAN TO LOSE THEIR POPULARITY

Upstairs,
Downstairs,"

popular BBC series, was big hit on public television.

In an intimate June affair before 23,000 close personal friends at Madison Square Garden, rock icon Sly Stone married 21-year-old Kathy Silva. Plans were to release 500 doves at the magic moment, but the Humane Society complained.

notable weddings of 1974

milestones

Meredith Baxter, 27, and David Birney, 34, stars of last season's hit series "Bridget Loves Bernie," about the marriage of a Catholic woman and a Jewish man. The wedding took place in a Presbyterian ceremony.

notable show biz birth

DEATHS

Samuel Goldwyn,
film mogul, died on January 31 at 91.

Chet Huntley,
cohost of "The Huntley-Brinkley Report," died on March 20 at 62 years of age.

William A. "Bud" Abbott,
one half of the comedy duo Abbott and Costello, died on April 24 at 78.

Edward "Duke" Ellington,
the jazz great, died on May 24 at 75.

Earl Warren,
former chief justice of the Supreme Court, died on July 9 at 83.

Cassandra "Mama Cass" Elliot
of The Mamas and Papas, choked on a ham sandwich on July 29, and died at 33.

Jacqueline Susann,
the bestselling novelist, famous for coining the phrase "Once Is Not Enough," died of cancer at the age of 53.

Walter Lippman,
the journalist, died on December 14 at age 85.

Jack Benny
died on December 27 at 80.

David Faustino, cheesehead son on TV's "Married...With Children," was born in California on March 3.

11

'74

1. **the way we were** Barbra Streisand
2. **seasons in the sun** Terry Jacks
3. **the streak** Ray Stevens
4. **(you're) having my baby** Paul Anka
5. **kung-fu fighting** Carl Douglas
6. **billy, don't be a hero** Bo Donaldson & The Heywoods
7. **annie's song** John Denver
8. **the loco-motion** Grand Funk Railroad
9. **tsop (the sound of philadelphia)** MFSB featuring The Three Degrees
10. **i can help** Billy Swan

hit music

THANKS TO ALBUMS BY FUTURE DISCO DONS K.C. AND TH
SUNSHINE BAND AND THE BEE GEES, THE FIRST STIRRING
OF THE DANCE MUSIC THAT WOULD DEFINE THE SECON
HALF OF THE SEVENTIES HIT THE AIRWAVES THIS YEA

bestselling

hardcover books cost from $8.95 to $10.00.

Capitalizing on their role in cracking the Watergate scandal, ace *Washington Post* reporters Carl Bernstein and Bob Woodward published **All the President's Men.** Some readers complained that, after finishing the whole thing, they still didn't know who Deep Throat was.

books

nonfiction

1. **how to be your own best friend**
   mildred newman & bernard berkowitz with jean owen

2. **the joy of sex**
   alex comfort

3. **you can profit from a monetary crisis**
   harry browne

4. **alistair cooke's america**
   alistair cooke

5. **plain speaking**
   merle miller

6. **times to remember**
   rose fitzgerald kennedy

7. **in one era and out the other**
   sam levenson

8. **alive: the story of the andes survivors**
   piers paul read

9. **all the president's men**
   carl bernstein & bob woodward

10. **upstairs at the white house**
    j. b. west

15

UCLA'S 7-YEAR WINNING STREAK WAS BROKEN
THIS YEAR WHEN NORTH CAROLINA SNAGGED THE
NCAA BASKETBALL CHAMPIONSHIP.

little league
baseball, inc.,

made two key moves this year: First
they decided to exclude foreign
teams from future Little League
World Series; then they decided to
include girl players on future Little
League teams.

**HANK AARON SURPASSED
BABE RUTH'S RECORD OF
714 HOME RUNS**

sports

In both baseball and football it was a
year of streaks. The Oakland A's won
the World Series for the 3rd straight
year, defeating the Los Angeles
Dodgers in 5 games. In football,
the Miami Dolphins defeated the
Minnesota Vikings 24–7 in the Super
Bowl, becoming only the second
team in gridiron history to take
the championship 2 years running.

Godfather 2 took most of the statues this year. Along with Best Picture, **Francis Ford Coppola** snagged Best Director and **Robert DeNiro** took Best Supporting Actor. Best Actor went to **Art Carney** for *Harry and Tonto*. **Ellen Burstyn** took Best Actress for *Alice Doesn't Live Here Anymore*. **Ingrid Bergman,** back on the big screen, received Best Supporting Actress for *Murder on the Orient Express*.

TOP 5 MOVIES

1. *The Towering Inferno,* 20th Century Fox/Warner Bros., $52,000,000
2. *Blazing Saddles,* Warner Bros., $47,800,000
3. *Young Frankenstein,* 20th Century Fox, $38,823,000
4. *Earthquake,* Universal, $35,849,994
5. *The Trial of Billy Jack,* Warner Bros., $31,100,000

It was the year of years for veteran comic talent Mel Brooks, who scored with monster movie parody **YOUNG FRANKENSTEIN** and oater send-up **BLAZING SADDLES.**

movies

'74

The Buick Skylark was named Consumer Reports Best Buy of the Year.

Catalytic converters became standard equipment on the majority of Detroit cars in an effort to meet stricter U.S. air pollution standards. The converter was designed to take the hydrocarbon particulates and carbon monoxide given off as exhaust and turn them into water and carbon dioxide, a relatively harmless alternative to polluting particulates.

wheels

In a classic BIG THREE car-maker move, Detroit tried to even up profits lost on large-car sales by upping the price of better-selling small cars. In some instances, subcompact cars were priced almost as much as midsize sedans.

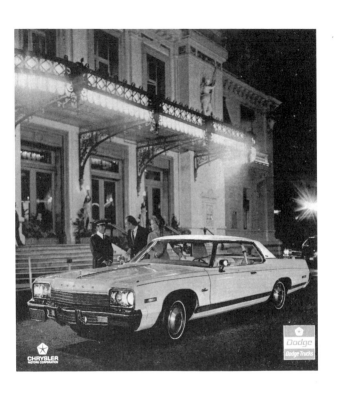

HAIRDRESSERS REJOICED AS THE FLAT, "LIMP" LOOK THAT DOMINATED THE EARLY PART OF THE DECADE BECAME FLUFFIER, MORE STYLED —THE BEGINNING OF THE "BIG HAIR" LOOK.

a paisley tie cost $6.50

Turquoise remained a popular accessory for men and women. A Navajo silver and turquoise bracelet cost $135.

surplice wrap...
in **Antron Nylon** and
spandex. 8-16.
At Robby Len's thoughtful
price, $21.

Swimagination.
It's what
you're all about.
Robby Len

fashion

"Streaking"

in which a participant unexpect
edly appeared nude and ran by a
group of clothed people, spread
from college campuses to public
parks, concerts and nationally
televised awards presentations.

final factoid

archive photos: inside front cover, pages 1, 3, 11, 16, inside back cover.

associated press: pages 2, 5, 6, 15, 25.

photofest: pages 8, 9, 10, 13, 18, 19.

original photography:
beth phillips: pages 21, 22, 23.

photo research:
alice albert

coordination:
rustyn birch

design:
carol bokuniewicz design
ginger krantz

"74